MOTHER STORIES FROM THE BOOK OF MORMON

―――――――――

By
William A. Morton

Copyright © 2016 Read Books Ltd.
This book is copyright and may not be
reproduced or copied in any way without
the express permission of the publisher in writing

British Library Cataloguing-in-Publication Data
A catalogue record for this book is available from
the British Library

CONTENTS

LEHI AND HIS FAMILY. 5
HOW NEPHI GOT THE GOOD BOOK. 9
HOW NEPHI GOT THE GOOD BOOK. 12
HOW THE LORD ANSWERED NEPHI'S PRAYER. 15
HOW THE LORD GUIDED LEHI AND HIS FAMILY. 18
WHAT HAPPENED ON A HUNTING TRIP. 21
NEPHI AS A SHIP BUILDER. 25
WHAT TOOK PLACE ON THE GREAT WATERS. 29
LEHI AND HIS PEOPLE
IN THE PROMISED LAND.................................32
THE NEPHITES AND THE LAMANITES. 36
ZENIFF AND HIS PEOPLE.................................39
HOW THE PEOPLE OF ZENIFF WERE
BROUGHT INTO BONDAGE...............................42
HOW THE LORD DELIVERED HIS PEOPLE.. 46
REMARKABLE CONVERSIONS AND
MISSIONARY EXPERIENCE. 50
MISSION OF THE SONS OF MOSIAH TO THE LAMANITES. ...55
SAMUEL THE LAMANITE—HIS PROPHECIES
AND THEIR FULFILLMENT................................59
TWO MEMORABLE BATTLES. 63
CHRIST'S VISIT TO THE NEPHITES. 67
THE THREE NEPHITES. 70
THE REIGN OF PEACE....................................72
THE LAST OF THE NEPHITES.............................74

LEHI AND HIS FAMILY.

So you want me to tell you a story, children. I will gladly do so, for when I was a child like one of you, I loved to listen to stories, too—stories about great and good men and women, and good boys and girls.

The story I am going to tell you this evening is about a good man named Lehi, and his family, who lived many, many years ago in a country far across the sea.

Lehi had a good wife. Her name was Sariah. They had four sons. Their names were Laman, Lemuel, Sam and Nephi. Nephi and Sam were very good boys. They loved their father and mother and were always obedient to them.

But Laman and Lemuel were not at all like their brothers. They did not obey their parents, but often vexed them by doing things that were wrong.

That was displeasing to our Heavenly Father, and He did not love Laman and Lemuel as He loved Sam and Nephi.

The people who lived in the same place as Lehi were wicked. They would not do as the Lord wished, so He said He would have to punish them, to teach them to do better. He told Lehi to go out among them, and to tell them that if they did not stop doing wicked things, He would not bless them as He had done, but would let people from another country come and take them away to be their servants.

Lehi preached many times to the people, but not one of them would believe what he said. Then the Lord told Lehi to gather his family together, and He would lead them to a new and beautiful country, far across great waters. That was to this land in which we now live.

Lehi did as the Lord told him. He left his home and all his

riches, and, with his wife and children, started out for the strange land which the Lord had told him about.

I suppose you would like to know how they traveled. Well, I believe they rode on camels. Camels can travel fast and carry heavy loads. Some of them can travel one hundred miles in a day.

There were no houses in the part of the country through which Lehi and his family traveled, so they took tents with them to live in. One day they came to a large river of water. It ran through a beautiful valley. By the side of the river they put up their tents. Then they knelt in prayer, and Lehi gave thanks to God for having taken care of them on the way.

Lehi called the river Laman and the valley he called Lemuel. You know why he gave them those names. Yes, those were the names of his two elder sons.

I told you that Laman and Lemuel were disobedient boys. They were also unkind to their brothers. Their father, Lehi, would often sit down and talk kindly to them. He would plead with them to be good boys. He would tell them that if they would do right, and obey their parents, the Lord would love and bless them; but that He would not do so if they kept on grumbling and getting angry with their brothers.

Then Laman and Lemuel would say to their father, "We don't want to go to a new country. We want to go back to our old home and stay with the people there."

And their father would say, "but you know, my boys, the people there are not good; they do not do as our Heavenly Father wishes them, and He is going to punish them. That is why He told us to come away from them. If we had stayed there after the Lord told us to leave we should be punished also."

Then Nephi would say, "Yes, brothers, that is true. Now, let us be good boys, and do what the Lord and our parents tell us, and after a while we will get to a beautiful country, and we shall be far better and happier than we should be if we were to go back to the place we have left."

But Laman and Lemuel would not do as their father and brothers pleaded with them to do, and you will hear later what happened to them.

HOW NEPHI GOT THE GOOD BOOK.

One night as Lehi lay asleep on his bed in the tent, he heard a voice speak to him. It was the voice of the Lord out of heaven. The Lord said, "Lehi, I want you to get Laman, Lemuel, Sam and Nephi to go back to the place where they used to live and to bring back with them a wonderful book which a man has locked up in his home there."

"What is the name of the man who has the book?" Lehi asked.

"His name is Laban," said the Lord, "and I do not want him to have the book, for he does not do what the good book tells him to do."

"What is in the book?" Lehi asked.

"It is a very precious history," said the Lord. "It tells of God and of many wonderful things which He has done. I want you to get the book and to take it with you to the promised land, so that your children may be taught the commandments of God."

The next morning Lehi told Laman, Lemuel, Sam and Nephi all that the Lord had told him about the wonderful book. How happy Nephi and Sam felt as they listened to what their father said. Then said Nephi, "Yes, father, we will go and get the book; and when we come back you will read to us some of the wonderful things recorded in it."

"I will, my son," said the father. "But what is the matter with Laman and Lemuel?" asked Lehi, as he turned to his two elder sons.

O, how cross they looked as they said to their father, "We don't want to go for the book. We don't believe we could get it. We feel sure Laban would not let us have it, and perhaps he would whip us for coming for it."

"We are not afraid of Laban," said Nephi and Sam. "The Lord has told us to do this, and we know He will take care of us. He would not want us to go if He did not know that we could get the book."

"That is right," said the father. "If you will do what the Lord wants you to do, all will be well."

After a while Laman and Lemuel agreed to go with their brothers. But they did not believe they would get the book. It was a long journey to Laban's home, and the boys were glad when they came in sight of it.

"Now, who is to go and try to get the book?" asked Laman, the eldest son.

"I will tell you what we will do," said Nephi. "We will cast lots, and the one on whom the lot falls will go to Laban and ask him for the book."

They all agreed to that. The lot fell upon Laman, so he set out for Laban's home. For a long time his brothers watched for him to come back. At last they saw him. He came running away from Laban's house.

"Oh, dear!" exclaimed Nephi, "Laman has not got the book!"

They sat in silence till their brother came up to them. His face was very pale and he was trembling with excitement. He was also very angry.

Going over to Nephi, he said, with a loud voice, "I told you before we started that we would not get the book, but you would not believe me. Do you believe me now?"

"We are sorry," said Nephi, "that your visit to Laban was in vain. Will you please tell us why you failed to get the book?"

"When I told Laban what I wanted," said Laman, "he became very angry. He called me a thief and a robber, and said if I did not leave his house at once he would kill me. He reached for his sword, and I had to run as fast as I could to save my life. Come, let us go back to our father."

"No," said Nephi, "I am not going to give up with one trial. I still believe we will get the book."

"O, you do," said Laman, and he turned up his nose in a sneering way. "Pray, how do you hope to get the book when I could not get it?"

"I believe the Lord will help us to get it," said Nephi. "I have just thought of a plan, and if you boys will help me carry it out, it may be the means of getting us the book."

"Well, let us hear your plan," said Laman.

"It is this," said Nephi: "that we go down to the place where we used to live, get all the money our father left there, and come back and offer it to Laban for the book."

"That is a good idea," said Sam. "I am ready to go."

"I like the plan, too," said Lemuel. "Come, Laman, let us go and try it."

So the boys started for the home in which they used to live. Tomorrow evening I will tell you the rest of the story.

HOW NEPHI GOT THE GOOD BOOK.

On arriving at their home, Nephi and his brothers got all the money and put it into a large bag. Then they prepared a lunch with some of the food they had brought with them, and when they had finished the meal, they took up the bag of money and set out for Laban's home.

Now, Laban loved money very much, and when he saw the large bag of gold and silver his eyes sparkled with delight. "If I could get that bag of money," he thought, "I would be one of the richest men in the country."

But he did not want to give the book for it. No, he wanted to keep the book and the money, too. The boys sat waiting for Laban to go and get them the book. Suddenly he jumped up and gave a loud call for his servants, and when they came running into the room he told them that Laman, Lemuel, Sam and Nephi had tried to rob him. Laban and the servants seized their swords and ran at the boys, trying to kill them. The boys ran quickly out of the house, leaving the bag of money behind them. Laban got it and kept it. Nephi and his brothers ran over the hills till they came to some large rocks, and there they hid themselves. Laban and his servants followed them a long way, and when they saw they could not catch them they returned home.

Failing to get the book, and seeing that they had lost all their money, Laman and Lemuel became very angry. They put all the blame on Nephi and Sam, and seizing two large branches of a tree, they began to beat their younger brothers with them. Nephi and Sam pleaded with their brothers to stop beating them, but they would not.

Just then Nephi saw a bright light coming down from heaven, and a moment later a beautiful angel, dressed in a shining, white robe, stood before them.

"You are very bad boys," the angel said to Laman and Lemuel. "The Lord is displeased with you because of the way you have treated your brothers. He has sent me to tell you that He will not bless you as He has done, and that He will give many good things to Sam and Nephi."

The angel told Nephi to dry his tears, and not to fear, for the Lord would help him to get the good book.

When Laman and Lemuel saw the angel they were frightened. They said they were sorry for having beaten their brothers, and that they would not do so again. They asked Nephi and Sam to forgive them. They did so freely.

Nephi then told his brothers to stay behind while he made another effort to get the book. It was almost dark at the time, so, without being seen, he made his way towards Laban's home. As he neared the place he saw a man lying upon the ground. He went over to him, and was greatly surprised to find that the man was Laban. Laban had drunk a great deal of wine that evening.

As Nephi stood looking at Laban, the voice of the Lord spoke to him, telling him to dress himself in Laban's clothes and to go to Laban's home and get the good book.

Nephi did as the Lord told him. On reaching the home of Laban he was met by one of the servants. Nephi told the servant to go and get the good book and to follow him. The servant did as he was told, thinking all the while that Nephi was his master, Laban, and that he was taking the book out to read to the people.

When Laman, Lemuel and Sam saw Nephi coming towards them, they were very much frightened and began to run away. They thought it was Laban; for, as I told you, Nephi had dressed himself in Laban's clothing.

Nephi called to his brothers to wait, and when they heard his voice they turned and came towards him.

Zoram (that was the name of Laban's servant) was greatly surprised at that moment. He saw that Nephi was not his master, and he was about to run back home when Nephi caught him by the arm.

"Do not have the least fear, Zoram," said Nephi. "The Lord has told us to do this, and if you will come down with us to our father and mother we will treat you kindly, and will take you with us to a beautiful country far across the great waters."

Zoram agreed to go with Nephi and his brethren. So, with the good book safe in their hands, they started back for the place where their father and mother were watching and waiting for them.

On seeing his sons coming, Lehi hastened to meet them, and when he heard that they had the good book with them he shed tears of joy. That evening they all knelt in prayer, and Lehi thanked and praised the Lord for bringing his boys back safely. Then he opened the book and read to them some of the wonderful things which the Lord had done from the creation of the world.

HOW THE LORD ANSWERED NEPHI'S PRAYER.

I am going to tell you this evening about another trip which Nephi and his brethren made to Jerusalem, the city where they came from, and what took place on the way back.

You see, the country they were going to was a very large country. There were no people living in it at that time. But the Lord wanted it filled with good men and women and good boys and girls.

So He told Lehi to send his sons back to Jerusalem to ask a man named Ishmael and his family, who lived there, to go with them to the wonderful country far across the great waters.

Ishmael had a number of beautiful daughters, and the Lord wanted Lehi's sons to marry some of them, so that they could have good families.

Lehi told his sons what the Lord wanted them to do, and they all said they would go. After traveling for a long time they arrived at the home of Ishmael. They were taken in and were treated very kindly.

Nephi told Ishmael why he and his brethren had come to his home. Then they all talked the matter over, and at last Ishmael and his family said they would go with Nephi and his brethren.

A day or two later the company started out for the place where Lehi and his wife were. All went well for a time; but after a while Laman and Lemuel and part of Ishmael's family stopped and said they would go no farther.

Nephi pleaded with them to continue the journey. He told them that if they would do as the Lord wanted them to do, He would take them across the great waters and land them safely in a beautiful country, where they would find all manner of choice fruit and other good things.

"We don't want to go to a new country," they answered, sharply. "We want to go back to our own home, and stay with the people there."

"Well," said Nephi, "you can go back if you want to, but if you do you will be sorry. The people you speak of are wicked, and the Lord is going to punish them. So if you go back you will be punished, too."

Then Laman spoke very sharply to Nephi. "We do not believe you," he said. "How do you know that the Lord is going to punish the people in the place where we used to live?"

"He told our father so," said Nephi, "and everything that the Lord says is true. You did not believe we would get the good book our father sent us for, but we did get it, just as the Lord said we would."

Then Laman and Lemuel and some of Ishmael's family grew very angry. They ran and caught Nephi and tied him with strong cords to a tree.

"You will not preach to us any more," they said. "We are going to go away and leave you here, and after a while wild beasts will come and kill and eat you."

Poor Nephi! What a terrible way to be treated by his own brothers! He was suffering great pain, for the cords were cutting his wrists and ankles. But he did not get angry, nor speak hard words to those who had so cruelly treated him. He knew the Lord would not let the wild beasts harm him, and after a time He would help him to get free.

A happy thought came to him: he would pray to the Lord to give him strength to break the cords. He looked up to heaven and said, "Dear Heavenly Father, I know you will not let me be left here to be killed by wild beasts. Please give me strength to break these cords, that I may be able to go back to my dear father and mother."

At that moment Nephi felt great strength come into his body. The Lord had heard and answered his prayer. He broke the cords as easily as if they had been tiny threads and stood forth free before his brethren.

When they saw what had happened, they began to tremble with fear. "Surely, the Lord is with Nephi," they said, and they came and bowed down before him and begged of him to forgive them.

What did Nephi do? He said, "My dear brothers, I freely forgive you for all the wrong you have done me. Now pray to our Father in Heaven to forgive you also."

They did so, and then the company began to travel again. They reached home in safety. Nephi and his brothers married four of the daughters of Ishmael, and after a time little baby boys and girls were born to them.

HOW THE LORD GUIDED LEHI AND HIS FAMILY.

This evening I am going to tell you how Lehi and his family were guided on their journey.

They were now a long way from their old home. They had not been in that part of the land before, and the place was new and strange to them. They could not ask anyone to tell them the way they should travel, for, as I told you, there was no one living in that part.

How were they to know which way they should go?

"I can see what is going to happen to us," said Laman one evening as they all sat outside their tents.

Nephi was reading the good book at the time, but on hearing what his brother said he stopped. Looking straight into the face of Laman, he asked, "What do you think is going to happen to us?"

"We are going to get lost; that is what is going to happen," said Laman, sharply.

"I don't think so," said Nephi, calmly, and a bright smile lit up his sweet face. "I am sure we will get to the wonderful country all right."

"O, yes," said Laman, as he cast a wicked glance at Nephi, "you are sure of everything. You know all and we know nothing. Isn't that so, boys?" he asked, turning to his other brothers and to the sons of Ishmael.

They all, with the exception of Sam, nodded their heads, which meant that they agreed with what Laman had said.

Then Sam spoke up in behalf of his brother: "I think," said he, "that you are all too hard on Nephi. It is a shame the way you have treated him. He is one of the best boys that ever lived, and I am proud to have him for my brother."

"Well, you won't feel so proud of him after a while," said Lemuel, "when he leads you away over those mountains and you get lost."

"Do not be afraid, Sam," said Nephi. "We will find the way all right."

"I know we will," said Sam, "and I will follow you, Nephi, wherever you go."

"And how do you know you will find the way?" Laman asked, turning to his brother Sam.

"I believe the Lord will show us the way," said Sam. "Indeed, I know He will, if we will have faith in Him and do what He tells us from time to time."

"That is true," said Nephi. "And now I want to tell you what I have just read in the good book. After Moses had led the children of Israel out of Egypt they came to the waters of the Red Sea. On looking back they saw Pharaoh and his army coming after them.

"'Oh, dear, what shall we do?' they cried. 'We cannot cross these waters. In a little while we will all be killed.'

"Then Moses stood up before them and said, 'Do not be afraid. The Lord will save yon from Pharaoh's army.' Then he stretched his rod across the waters, the sea divided, and all the children of Israel crossed over on dry ground. When they had reached the other side, Moses stretched forth his rod again, the waters came back and drowned Pharaoh and all his soldiers.

"Now, the lesson we can learn from this," Nephi added, "is that as the Lord led the children of Israel out of Egypt and through the Red Sea, so He can lead us to the beautiful country He has told us about."

"That is a very good lesson, Nephi," said his father. "I am sure the Lord will guide us right. Let us now go into our tents and offer up our prayers before we retire to rest."

Nephi was the first to awake in the morning. He arose quietly and dressed himself. He decided to go out for a walk in the fresh air, and listen to the birds sing their sweet songs in the trees.

As he stepped outside the tent, to his great surprise he saw a large ball lying on the ground. He ran and picked it up. It was not like any other ball he had ever seen. It was made of fine brass, and it had two hands, like the hands of a watch.

He went quickly into the tent and awoke his father. "Look, father dear," he said, "at the beautiful brass ball I found lying outside our tent this morning."

Lehi took the ball and examined it carefully. As he looked at it one of the hands began to point in a certain direction.

"See, Nephi!" he exclaimed, "the hands are moving."

"So they are," said Nephi. "What a wonderful ball this is!"

Then all the rest of the company were awakened and shown the wonderful ball. As they looked on it with wondering eyes, Lehi said, "We need fear no longer, for if we are faithful the hands on the ball will point out to us the way we should go."

And so they did.

Where do you think the wonderful ball came from?

WHAT HAPPENED ON A HUNTING TRIP.

With the wonderful brass ball to guide them, Lehi, his family and the rest of the company took up their tents and started to travel again. It was a pretty sight to see them all in line crossing the river Laman.

When they had traveled for many days they decided to stop again for a short time. So they chose a cool place, by the side of a stream of clear, sparkling water, and there they put up their tents.

That evening Nephi and his brothers and the sons of Ishmael began to make preparations for a hunting trip, which they had decided to take the following morning. They were not going out to hunt for pleasure. No, it was for the purpose of getting food, for the only food the company had at that time was wild fruit and the flesh of wild animals.

I am sure you could not guess what kind of weapons they had. "Guns?"

No, there were no guns in those days. They used bows and arrows, slings and stones. Some of the bows were made of wood and some of steel. Nephi had a good, steel bow. He and his brothers had practiced so much with their bows and arrows and slings that they were very good shots, but Nephi was the best of all. He could hit the mark almost every time.

Early the next morning the party of young hunters started off in search of food. They took the brass ball with them to point the way. They traveled for a long time without seeing an animal fit to kill.

At last they stopped suddenly. What was the noise they heard a short distance ahead of them? It was made by a fine, large animal, that jumped up frightened and started to run as the hunters drew near. It ran to the top of a small hill, and there it stood looking back at Nephi and his brethren.

Nephi quickly drew an arrow and placed it in his bow. He took good aim, and was just going to send the arrow through the air when his beautiful, steel bow broke in two. At the same moment the animal started to run again and was soon lost to sight.

Poor Nephi! How sorry he felt as he looked down at his broken bow. Then he cast a glance at Laman, and saw that his face was pale with anger. He wished he had let one of the others shoot, but it was now too late to mend matters.

Laman turned to Nephi and began to scold him. He was quickly stopped by Sam, who said sharply: "It is unkind of you to speak that way to Nephi. He did not break his bow wilfully. It was an accident. And he feels bad enough over it without you hurting his feelings more by abusing him. Let us say no more about the matter, but go on our way."

All day long they hunted without killing a single animal. When evening came the party, with the exception of Nephi and Sam, started back for their tents.

"I do not care to go home yet," Nephi said. "I will follow you later."

"I am going to stay with Nephi," said Sam. "Tell father and mother we will be home before midnight."

After Laman and Lemuel and the sons of Ishmael had left, Nephi turned to Sam and said:

"Sam, I tell you what we will do; we will kneel down and pray to our Heavenly Father to help us get some food. I am sure He will do so."

"So am I," said Sam. "He has helped us many times before."

The two young men went over and knelt down under a large tree, where they prayed earnestly to God to help them get food for the company. I will tell you presently how their prayer was answered.

The other members of the hunting party returned to camp and told what had happened. Their story cast a gloom over the whole company.

"What a terrible state to be in!" exclaimed one of the daughters of Ishmael. "There is barely enough food for another meal. When that is gone, starvation will stare us in the face."

Lehi and his wife Sariah were sitting together with bowed heads a short distance away. Tears were running down the poor mother's cheeks. She was not crying because the food supply had almost run out. No, she was thinking of her boys, Nephi and Sam, out in the mountains alone, in danger of being killed by wild beasts, and the darkness of night fast coming on.

Lehi took her hand in his and in a comforting voice said: "Fear not, Sariah, the Lord will watch over and protect our boys. I believe they will soon return, and that they will bring food with them."

On hearing that, Nephi's mother dried her tears, and turning to her husband, said: "Thank you, Lehi, for those words. I will trust in God to bring our sons back safely."

Let us now go back to Nephi and Sam.

When they had ceased praying, Nephi sat down and quickly made a new bow out of a branch of a tree. Then they walked briskly to the top of a hill a short distance away.

At the foot of the hill lay a fertile valley, with a stream of clear, cool water running gently through it. Birds were singing their evening songs in the trees all around, and the air was filled with the fragrance of wild flowers, which grew in abundance on the hillside.

For a moment Sam and Nephi stood gazing in admiration on the beautiful scene before them. Then they began to descend the hill. As they were nearing the foot they saw a sight which made them stop suddenly. At the other side of the stream, not far from where they stood, they beheld two fine, big animals quenching their thirst. Quick as a shot Nephi and Sam dropped to the ground. Placing an arrow in each of their bows, they took aim and fired. The arrows flew straight to the mark and the animals fell.

With thankful hearts the young hunters dashed through the stream, and on reaching the opposite bank, looked down upon the fine animals they had slain. Here was meat to last the company several days. Cutting down two large branches from a tree, they fastened the beasts upon them and started for the tents of their father.

What a look of surprise came over the faces of Laman and Lemuel and the sons of Ishmael when Nephi and Sam came into camp late that evening.

Lehi heard his sons coming and went out to meet them, and as he beheld the two fine animals, he took Sam and Nephi by the hands and said: "I knew, my sons, that you would not come back without food. The Lord always provides for His faithful children."

NEPHI AS A SHIP BUILDER.

My story this evening is about the same people I told you of in my other stories—Lehi and his followers.

How many years, do you think, those people spent in traveling through the country? Eight. That is a long time—almost as long as some of you have lived on the earth.

One day, at the end of the eighth year, they came to a very beautiful and fruitful part of the country. How happy they all felt! On every side there were trees and bushes laden with choice, wild fruit. But that was not all. There was also a large number of natural bee-hives, almost all of them filled with delicious honey.

The entire company stood for a time gazing in silence on the scene before them. Then they began to gather fruit and honey, and when they had collected a good supply, they sat down and began to feast.

"This," said Nephi, "is one of the best meals we have had since we left home eight years ago."

"Isn't this honey delicious?" said Lemuel.

"It is," said his father.

That evening as they all sat in front of their tents, watching the sun go down behind the hills, Lehi said, "This is a very rich part of the country. I have been trying all day to think of a name by which to call it, and I think I have the right name at last."

"And what is the name, father dear?" asked Nephi's wife, a daughter of Ishmael.

"Bountiful," Lehi answered.

"The proper name!" they all shouted in chorus. So the place was given the name Bountiful.

After Lehi and his people had rested for a short time, they began to travel again. Nephi and Sam—they were always together—rode ahead of the company. On reaching the top of a high hill they stopped suddenly. They sat gazing for a few moments at the scene before them. Then they turned and started at a quick pace for the rest of the party.

"What can be the matter?" Lehi asked, as he saw his two sons coming back.

As Nephi and Sam came near the party, Nephi put his hand to his mouth and shouted as loudly as he could, "The great waters! The great waters!" On hearing that, every one in the company became excited, and all hurried forward to get a look at the mighty ocean.

What strange feelings came into the hearts of Lehi and his followers as they looked out upon the sea. How were they to cross such a large body of water?

Just then Laman spoke. "It seems to me," said he, "that it is now time for us to turn and go back home. I have felt from the day we started that we would have to turn back some time. That time has come at last."

"And I have felt from the day we started," said Nephi, in a calm but firm voice, "that we would never go back to our old home again. I know that God is in heaven. I know He led the children of Israel through the Red Sea and I know that He can and will carry us across these mighty waters."

On hearing that, Laman and Lemuel and some of the sons and daughters of Ishmael began to laugh and to make fun of Nephi.

"So you think God is going to come down out of heaven and carry us in His arms across this great ocean," said Lemuel, "and set us down in a wonderful country on the other side."

"No," said Nephi, "I do not think anything of the kind. But I do believe He will tell us how we can cross these waters."

Then Lehi, their father, spoke. "My sons," he said, "do not get angry with each other. Remember you are brothers. Remember, also, Laman, that the Lord can do great things. He made this world in which we live. Surely, then, He can help us to get to the other side of this ocean. Now, let me tell you what I want you and the rest of the company to do: I want you to gather all the fruit and honey you can. We must collect a big supply, for it will be many days before we get to the new country."

"So you think we shall get across these great waters?" said Laman to his father.

"I am sure we will," said Lehi. "Now, let us get to work."

All day long they gathered choice fruit and honey, and when the evening came they sat down and looked with great satisfaction upon the labors of their hands.

Nephi arose early the next morning. He looked pale, and it was easily to be seen that he had some great matter upon his mind. He had slept very little, but had spent the greater part of the night wondering how the company could get across the great waters. He went to the tent in which his parents were sleeping and gently woke his father. "I am going into the mountains, father," he said, "to spend the day in prayer. I feel that I shall have good news for you when I come back."

His father raised himself, and putting his arm around his son's neck, drew him to him. Then he kissed him and said, "May God Bless you, my son, and answers the prayers you offer up to Him this day."

After traveling for a long time, Nephi reached the top of a very high mountain. All was quiet and peaceful around him. He sat down and rested a little while. Then he knelt in prayer. He prayed to God with all his heart to show him how the company could get across the great waters. I believe he prayed three times. Then something very wonderful happened. The Lord showed to Nephi in a vision a picture of a ship. It was not like any other ship he had ever seen.

As Nephi gazed in wonder upon the vessel, the Lord said to him, "Nephi, I want you to build a ship like this one, to carry your company across the great waters."

"But, Lord," said Nephi, "I do not know how to build a ship."

"I know that," said the Lord, "but I will teach you. You will come up into this mountain often and pray to me, and I will show you how to build the ship."

The Lord then told Nephi where he could get one with which to make tools, and after giving him other instructions, He told him to return and tell his people all that he had seen and heard.

At first Laman and Lemuel and the sons of Ishmael would not believe him. They made great fun of him, saying he would never be able to build a ship. But after Nephi had talked very seriously to them, they started to help him. Piece after piece was added to the vessel, and after a long time the ship was finished and ready to be launched.

In my next story I shall tell you what happened soon after the company had set out across the great waters.

WHAT TOOK PLACE ON THE GREAT WATERS.

The morning after the ship was finished all the company came together to look at it. It was a very fine vessel. Nephi and those who had assisted him were well pleased with their labors. They had built the ship exactly as the Lord had told them, and had done their work well.

Then Lehi turned to his four sons and also to the sons of Ishmael and said, "You have our grateful thanks for the great work which you have done. You have built a splendid vessel, and I am sure it will carry us safely across these great waters to the promised land."

A busy time followed. The men and women worked hard all day carrying meat, fruit and honey down into the ship, and their little sons and daughters helped them.

When night came they were all pretty tired; but they did not seem anxious to go to sleep. That was the last night they would spend on land for a long time. On the morrow they would be out upon the great waters. Finally they retired, one by one, and the moon and stars shown brightly over the sleeping camp.

The company was up and at work early next morning. The women prepared breakfast and the men took down the tents and attended to other duties. Nephi and Sam and some of Ishmael's sons were busily employed at fixing the sails of the ship and getting the vessel ready for her first voyage.

At last the time came for all to go on board. A line was formed. Lehi and his wife, being the oldest, marched at the head. The others followed, according to their ages. A sharp breeze was blowing and the vessel tugged at its chains as if anxious to get away.

When all of the company were safely on board, Nephi loosed

the ship, the wind immediately filled its sails, and a moment later it was gliding swiftly through the water on its way to the promised land.

All went well the first day. And all would have gone well every other day if Laman and Lemuel and some of the sons and daughters of Ishmael had conducted themselves as they should have done.

The second day the company was on the water, Laman and Lemuel began to sing and dance and to act in a very rude manner. Some of Ishmael's sons and daughters joined them. Their conduct made Nephi feel very bad, and he reproved them sharply.

"How can you act in such a shameful manner," he said, "after having received so many blessings from the Lord? Have you forgotten how good He has been to us, how He provided us with food on our journey and taught us how to build this ship? I tell you, the Lord is looking down upon you. He is displeased with you because of your conduct, and if you do not stop and humble yourselves before Him, He will surely punish you."

Those words made Laman and Lemuel very angry. They rushed at Nephi, and seizing him by the arms, they thrust him back against the mast of the ship. Then they called to the sons of Ishmael to bring a rope quickly. Their command was obeyed, and they bound Nephi hand and foot to the mast. There they kept him all day, suffering great pain, for the rope cut deep wounds in his flesh.

It was a great trial to Lehi and his wife to see their dear son in such a terrible condition. They pleaded with Laman and Lemuel to release Nephi, but they would not. The tears and prayers of Nephi's wife likewise failed to soften their stony hearts.

Nephi bore his sufferings well. Not one murmuring word fell from his lips. When Laman and Lemuel and the sons of Ishmael mocked him, and said unkind things to him, he heeded them not. He tried to comfort his father and mother and loving wife by telling them that all would be well, that in time the Lord would help him to get free.

And the Lord did. How? Listen and I will tell you. Two or three days later dark clouds began to gather in the sky. A storm was coming. Suddenly a flash of lightning lit up the heavens. Then a terrible peal of thunder shook the vessel. The rain came down in torrents. Then the wind changed and the vessel began to be driven back towards land.

The storm grew worse every hour. The waves dashed fiercely against the vessel and at times swept over its deck. In the face of that awful tempest stood poor Nephi, tied hand and foot to the mast. For three days and nights the storm lasted, and all that time the vessel was being driven back.

On the morning of the fourth day a terrible wave struck the ship and almost turned it over. Some of the women began to scream with fright. Laman and Lemuel became alarmed also. They saw that the Lord was angry with them: that He had let the storm come upon them because of the way in which they had treated their brother Nephi. Then another angry wave burst over the vessel and almost buried it in the depths of the sea.

Believing they were about to be destroyed, Laman and Lemuel and the sons of Ishmael repented of what they had done. They went over to Nephi, untied the ropes which bound him and set him free.

Nephi was so weak that he could hardly stand upon his feet. He knelt down, and looking up towards heaven he prayed with all his heart to God to cause the storm to cease, and to change the course of the wind so that the vessel might sail towards the promised land.

To the astonishment of all the people, the storm suddenly ceased, the sea became calm, and the vessel started again on its journey across the great waters.

LEHI AND HIS PEOPLE IN THE PROMISED LAND.

Lehi and his people had been a long time upon the great ocean. They were very tired, for they had seen nothing but water for many days. Some of them had begun to murmur, and to wonder if they should ever set foot upon land again. Then something happened which brought joy to every heart.

It was early in the morning. All the company were asleep except Nephi and Sam. Nephi was steering the ship and Sam was standing in the fore part of the vessel looking over the great waters.

Suddenly Sam's quick eyes caught sight of a dark object. He stood still and held his breath. Could it be land? He looked again, and then he gave a shout for joy which startled the whole company. In a few moments men, women and children were by his side, asking what had happened. "Look!" he exclaimed, as he pointed across the waters. "See, yonder is the promised land!"

"It is, indeed!" they all shouted, and the children clapped their hands and cried, "Land! land! land!"

"The Lord's name be praised!" said Lehi when he heard the joyful news, although he could not see the land so far off, for he was old and his eyes had become dim.

After breakfast, all set to work making preparations for landing. The splendid little ship rode proudly as ever over the waves, and early in the afternoon Nephi steered the vessel safe to shore. When the company had landed they all knelt down upon the ground, and Lehi offered a prayer of thanksgiving and praise to God for having brought them to the promised land.

It was a beautiful country. The sun shone in its glory. The birds welcomed the company with their sweet songs, and the flowers delighted all with their rich perfume. On the hillsides animals of different kinds were feeding. Among them were horses, donkeys, cows and goats. There were also a great many wild fowl.

After breakfast the next morning, Lehi called the men of the company to him and said, "My sons, the first thing for us to do is to clear some land and plant the seed we have brought with us. The soil is very rich, and I am sure we shall reap excellent crops."

"That is just what we were going to do, father," said Nephi. "Come, brethren," he said to the others, "let us turn our attention to farming for a while."

Day after day the men worked in the fields. Each evening all the people met together and Nephi read to them out of the good book. Lehi also told them many wonderful things which the Lord had done. They felt very happy.

At last the seed was planted. Then the men went up into the hills and caught a number of horses, donkeys, cows, and goats. The animals were wild, but through kind treatment they soon became tame. The cows and goats gave milk, the horses hauled wood and did other work, and the donkeys carried the boys and girls on merry rides over the rolling prairie.

The crops sprang up and grew rapidly, and when the time came for harvesting there was plenty of food for man and beast.

And now I am going to tell you, children, about the last days of the Prophet Lehi. He had become old and feeble, and the time was fast drawing near when his spirit would leave this world and go to dwell with the righteous in the Paradise of God.

Two baby boys had been born to him on the journey to the promised land. Their names were Jacob and Joseph. They were good children, always kind and obedient to their parents. On beautiful, warm days they would take their father by the hand and lead him gently to a comfortable seat under the shade of a large tree. Then they would sit down on the grass at his feet and listen while he told them stories of wonderful things which had happened many years before.

One day Lehi sent word to all the people to come to him, that he might bless them before he died. When they had assembled, he blessed them in turn. He promised them many good things from the Lord if they would keep the commandments of God and love and help each other.

When Joseph, Lehi's youngest son, went in to receive his blessing his father drew him close to him. He looked into his sweet, innocent face a few seconds; then he pressed him to his bosom and placed a loving kiss upon his lips.

While being blessed by his father, Joseph saw how good the Lord had been to him, and when he was told of the great blessings which would be bestowed upon him because of his faithfulness, he bowed his head on his father's neck and wept.

"And now, my son," said Lehi, "I am going to tell you of a wonderful thing which the Lord has told me will take place many years from now."

Joseph wondered what it could be. "You have seen the book which your brother Nephi is writing." Joseph answered that he had. "Well," said his father, "that is a history. It is an account of what has taken place among us since the day we left our home up to the present time. After Nephi has finished writing in it, he will deliver the book to another good man, who will continue the history. When the second writer has finished his part, he will give the book to a third, and in this manner the history of the people will be kept for hundreds and hundreds of years. When it is finished, it will be the most precious and wonderful book ever written.

"And what will become of the book, father?" asked Joseph.

"I was just going to tell you," said Lehi.

Joseph drew closer, and looked anxiously into his father's face.

"When the book is finished," continued Lehi, "the last writer will hide it in a deep hole in the ground. He will do that because wicked men might get it and destroy it. The book will be kept hid in the earth for thousands of years."

"At last the time will come for the book to be brought forth again. Then the Lord will send an angel to a boy named Joseph, the same name that you bear. The heavenly messenger will tell

Joseph of the book and show him the place in which it will lie buried. A few years later the precious history will be taken from its hiding place and given to the boy Joseph. The Lord will help the boy to change the language of the book to suit the language of the people living at that time. Then the book will be published, men will carry it into all the world, and the people of every nation will learn of the great things which the Lord will have done for us and our children."

"That is really wonderful," said Joseph. "It is, indeed," said his father. Then Lehi kissed his boy again and said, "May the Lord bless you, my son, forever."

Can my children tell me how the words of Lehi were fulfilled concerning the book that was to be hid in the ground?

THE NEPHITES AND THE LAMANITES.

I am going to tell you this evening what took place soon after the death of Lehi. Laman and Lemuel grew more wicked every day. Their hearts were full of hatred towards Nephi and Sam.

One evening they went off by themselves. They sat down under a large tree and talked together for a long time. I am sure you could not guess what they were doing. They were making plans to kill Sam and Nephi. Laman and Lemuel thought that if Nephi and Sam were dead the people would choose them to be their leaders.

They did not seem to know that the Lord was looking down upon them and listening to their wicked plot. But the Lord had seen and heard all, and He at once prepared a way for the escape of Nephi and Sam.

That night the Lord told Nephi to gather together all the people that wished to follow him and to take them away into another part of the country. All the good people agreed to go with Nephi and Sam, the wicked ones decided to stay with Laman and Lemuel.

Nephi and his people were guided on their way by the wonderful brass ball which I told you about in one of my other stories. After traveling many days they came to a place where they decided to settle.

"What shall we call this place?" asked one of the company.

Several voices answered at once: "We will call it Nephi, after our faithful leader." So the place was named Nephi. From that time all the people that followed Nephi were called Nephites. Those who stayed behind with Laman and Lemuel were called Lamanites.

Now that they were away from their wicked brethren, Nephi and his people felt very happy. They had brought with them many kinds of seed, so they laid out farms and gardens and planted the seed in them. God blessed their labors. His gentle rains and warm sun caused the seed to grow and to produce splendid crops, so that there was plenty of food for all.

In the evenings, when their work was done, the people would meet together, and Nephi would read to them out of the good book. Then they would pray to God, thanking Him for all His blessings, and asking Him to protect them from the wicked Lamanites.

At first they had only tents to live in, but after a while they took down their tents and put up beautiful houses in their place. In the course of a few years a splendid little city had sprung up in that desert region.

One Sabbath day, when the people had gathered together to worship God, Nephi asked them if they would like to build a beautiful temple to the Lord. They all said they would love to do so. A few days later a choice place was selected, and a number of men began to lay the foundation of the Lord's House. The hearts of the people swelled with joy as they saw the walls of the sacred building rise higher and higher. At last the temple was finished. The Lord was well pleased with it, and when the people went into the temple to worship Him He bestowed great blessings upon them.

One day all the people assembled together. They sent for Nephi, and when he arrived they told him that, because he had been such a good man, and had done so much for them, they had decided to make him their king.

But Nephi would not agree to such a thing. He said he did not wish to be king over them; that he wanted to be like one of themselves, and that he would continue to be their leader and teacher.

I must now take you back to Laman and Lemuel, and to the people who stayed with them. They, as I told you, were called Lamanites. O, dear, what a difference there was between them and the people of Nephi! What do you think had happened to Laman and the people who had stayed with him? The displeasure of the Lord had come upon them so that their skins had become dark, and they were fast becoming a wild and savage people. They had neither farms nor gardens, nor houses to live in. The only food they had to eat was fish and the flesh of wild beasts, and at night they slept in old, worn out tents. They had become dirty, idle, and lazy, just like the Indians we sometimes see going round begging food. Such, dear children, was the terrible condition into which the Lamanites were brought because of their disobedience to the commandments of God.

ZENIFF AND HIS PEOPLE.

Nephi lived with his people and taught them for many years. They all loved him, for he was a wise and a godly man, and had done many great things for them.

At last he became old and feeble. He knew that he had but a short time to live, so he took the history he had written and gave it to his brother Jacob. Then he chose a good man to reign as king over the Nephites.

Soon after that, Nephi died and his spirit went to Paradise to live with the righteous ones who had gone before.

One day, long after the death of Nephi, a man named Zeniff called together a number of his Nephite brethren. He told them he wanted to go and see how the Lamanites were getting on. "How many of you are willing to go with me?" he asked. Nearly all of them agreed to go. They began at once to make preparations for the trip. When the time came for them to leave, they bade their loved ones good-bye and set out on their journey.

After traveling many days, they came to the place where the Lamanites were. It was a fine country. Zeniff and those who were with him felt they would like to live there if the Lamanites would be willing for them to do so.

After resting awhile, Zeniff took four men and went into the city to see the king of the Lamanites. The king received his visitors kindly. Zeniff told the king that he and his brethren who were with him would like to remain in that part of the land.

King Laman said he would be pleased to have them stay, and that he would get the Lamanites who were in two of the cities to leave them and go to other places, so that the Nephites might go in and live in those cities.

You may think that that was a very kind act of the Lamanite king; but when I tell you what his object was, you will not think so kindly of him. He wanted the Nephites to go in and build up the cities, to cultivate the land and raise good crops. "When they have done that," said the king to himself, "I will get my army to come down and take the cities and the crops away from them. Then we will make the Nephites our servants."

The king of the Lamanites told Zeniff to bring his brethren and to settle in the land, and they did so.

Zeniff and his people began at once to improve the cities which the Lamanites had turned over to them. They planted crops of different kinds, also orchards and vineyards. Zeniff was a good man. He loved the Lord and kept His commandments and taught his people to do the same.

The Lord was pleased with them and gave them a great many good things. He blessed their farms so that they brought forth splendid crops. Their orchards yielded choice fruits in abundance, and their flocks and herds increased rapidly.

How little the Nephites knew at that time of the trouble which was soon to come upon them and of the great changes which a few years would bring about.

For some time the Lamanites had been watching the people of Zeniff. They saw their splendid crops, their sheep and cattle, and they longed to get possession of them. So they decided to make war upon the Nephites.

The Lamanites, when ready for battle, were a terrible-looking people. They were almost naked, and had the hair shaved off their heads. They were armed with bows and arrows, slings and stones, swords, and other weapons.

Zeniff, hearing that the Lamanites were going to attack his people, had the women and children taken away and hid in a safe place. Then he called all the men together and armed them for battle. The Nephites prayed mightily to the Lord to strengthen them, so that they might be able to defeat the Lamanites and thus be able to keep their homes and lands.

The Lord heard and answered the prayers of His people. The Lamanites fought like wild beasts, but were finally overcome.

Those who were not killed in battle fled back to their own lands, and the Nephites returned to their homes, their wives and children, praising God for the victory He had given them.

HOW THE PEOPLE OF ZENIFF WERE BROUGHT INTO BONDAGE.

While Zeniff was king over his people they were greatly blessed of the Lord. Zeniff had taught them to lead good lives and to be kind and helpful to each other.

The years passed by, Zeniff grew old and finally died. His son Noah began to reign in his stead. Noah was just as wicked as his father was good. He gathered around him many bad men. They flattered him and made him think he was a great man.

Noah built costly palace had horses and chariots and a large number of wives and servants. He led a shameful life, spending his days in feasting and in doing things which were exceedingly displeasing in the sight of the Lord. It required a great deal of money to support this ungodly king. He, therefore, put heavy taxes upon his people, and the Nephites had to work hard to pay the expenses of their wicked ruler.

One by one the Nephites began to follow the example of their king, and in the course of time the greater part of them had become almost as bad as Noah himself.

Now, there was a man among the Nephites who had watched with sorrow the conduct of his people. His name was Abinadi. He was a good man, and the Lord loved him.

One day the voice of the Lord came to Abinadi, saying, "Abinadi, I want you to go among this people and call them to repentance. Tell them that I, the Lord, am very angry with them because of their wickedness, and that if they do not cease doing evil, I will let the Lamanites come down upon them and overcome them, and they will become servants to the Lamanites."

Abinadi did as the Lord commanded him. He stood up in the midst of the Nephites and told them of the wicked things they had done, how angry the Lord was with them, and warned them of the trouble which would come upon them if they did not repent.

His words made them very angry. They rushed upon him, seized him, and marched him roughly to the king's court. They told Noah of the terrible things which Abinadi had prophesied would come upon the king and his people if they did not repent of their wickedness. "What shall we do with this man," they asked, "who has spoken such things against the king and against us?"

The cry went up, "Let him be put to death!" But Abinadi had not completed his mission, so the Lord delivered him out of their hands.

Two years later he appeared in their midst again. He began to preach with great power and courage. He repeated all that he had said before, and told them of the fate which awaited them if they refused to listen to the warning of the Lord.

O, foolish people! Instead of thanking the prophet for pointing out to them their errors, and for telling them how they could be saved from the judgments of God, they turned upon him with hearts full of anger, treated him in a shameful manner, and finally put him to death.

Among those who listened to the preaching of Abinadi was a young man named Alma. Alma believed what the prophet had said. He knew that he had spoken the truth. So Alma repented of his sins and began to live a godly life.

He wrote down all that Abinadi had said. Then he went quietly among the people and read to those who would listen to him the wonderful things which the prophet had spoken. Many believed the teachings of Alma. They repented also and commenced to serve the Lord. They had to be very careful.

They knew that if King Noah heard that they believed what Abinadi had said, he would have them put to death also. So on certain days they would go away out into the country, to a little forest, and there they would worship God and listen to the preaching of Alma.

In the forest there was a fountain of clear water, called the waters of Mormon. One day when all the believers were gathered together Alma asked them if they would like to be baptized, to show to the Lord that they were willing to serve Him and keep His commandments. They all clapped their hands for joy and said that that was what they desired. So Alma went down into the waters of Mormon and baptized them. Others were baptized from time to time, and finally the followers of Alma numbered four hundred and fifty.

It was too bad that poor Abinadi died without seeing the result of his labors. He had been the means of converting Alma, and Alma had converted four hundred and fifty people. Therefore, if Abinadi's life had been spared a few years longer his heart would have been made glad at seeing hundreds of his people forsake their evil ways and turn unto the Lord.

One day a man went to King Noah and told him that Alma had gathered a large number of people together and was advising them to turn against the king. That was not true, but the king believed it, and he at once sent out his army to destroy Alma and his people. But Alma heard of the coming of the army. He told the news to his followers and they quickly took down their tents and went away to another part of the country.

You will remember that Abinadi told the Nephites that if they did not stop doing wicked things the Lord would let the Lamanites come down upon them, conquer them and make them their servants. I will now tell you how the words of the prophet were fulfilled.

One day King Noah was up in a high tower. As he looked over the land he saw a sight which frightened him terribly—the armies of the Lamanites were coming to make war upon the Nephites! Noah ran down quickly out of the tower calling to his people to flee for their lives, as the Lamanites were coming to destroy them. Noah was a coward. He not only ran away himself, but told his men to leave their wives and children, so as to save their own lives.

Some of them did so, but the greater part of them stayed with their families. The cowardly Nephites who ran away were pursued by the Lamanites. A number of them were overtaken and slain.

When the Nephites who had stayed with their families saw the Lamanites coming towards them they sent out their fair daughters to plead with the Lamanites to spare their lives. The Lamanites were charmed with the beauty of the Nephite maidens. They told them not to fear, that they would neither hurt them nor their parents.

The Lamanites told the Nephites they would let them return to their homes and farms if they would agree to pay to the king of the Lamanites one-half of all their gold and silver and precious things, and also one-half of the crops which they might raise each year.

In order to save their lives the Nephites agreed to the demands of the Lamanites. That day the words of the Prophet Abinadi were fulfilled—the Nephites had become servants to the Lamanites.

"Did they remain all their lives in that condition?"

I will answer that question in my next story.

HOW THE LORD DELIVERED HIS PEOPLE.

At the close of my last story you asked me if the Nephites had to stay in bondage to the Lamanites all the rest of their lives. It will, I know, make you glad to hear that, in His own time, the Lord delivered them out of the hands of their oppressors.

But before setting them free. He permitted great afflictions to come upon them as punishment for their sins and to teach them to be humble and to live good lives.

As the years went by, the Lamanites treated the Nephites more cruelly. They made them go out and work in their fields, carry heavy burdens, and when they complained, the Lamanites beat them and told them to remember they were their servants.

There was a man reigning as king over the Nephites at that time, whose name was Limhi. He was the grandson of Zeniff. It made him feel very bad to look upon the afflictions of his people. But he could not help them, except by speaking kindly to them, telling them to bear their trials as patiently as possible, and to pray often and earnestly to the Lord to deliver them.

Three times the Nephites came to Limhi, saying, "O, king, we cannot stand the treatment of the Lamanites any longer. We would just as lieve die as continue to live in this condition. We want you to let us go to war with the Lamanites. We will fight with all our might to rid ourselves of this terrible slavery."

But Limhi knew that his people were weak and that they were far less in number than the Lamanites; so he advised them not to go to war. They kept on pleading with him, however, and, seeing that they were determined, he finally yielded.

The Nephites fought three battles with the Lamanites and each time the Nephites were badly beaten. Then they saw that no power save the power of God could deliver them; so they cried to the Lord in anguish of soul to help them to get free from their enemies.

At last the Lord heard and listened to their prayers. He saw that they were sorry for all the wicked things they had done, and for the way in which they had treated the Prophet Abinadi. So He looked down in mercy upon them and began to prepare a way for their escape. This is how He did it:

You remember that Zeniff and his followers left the rest of the Nephites to go up to the land of the Lamanites. The people whom Zeniff left were living in a city called Zarahemla. They had as their ruler a wise and good man named Mosiah. A number of times Mosiah's people had gone to him and said, "King Mosiah, what do you think has become of Zeniff and those who went with him to the land of the Lamanites? It is many years since they left us, and we have never heard from them."

And Mosiah would say, "I am sure, my people, I do not know what has become of them. I fear the Lamanites have slain them. It seems to me that if they were alive we would have heard from them."

One day, sixteen large, strong men went to King Mosiah and told him they had decided to go in search of the people of Zeniff. At first Mosiah refused to let them go: he was afraid they might get lost also. But after they had talked with him for some time he consented.

They chose for their leader a man named Ammon. He was a man of great strength and courage. So, with Amnion at their head, and provisions to last them a long time, the party set out in search of their brethren. A large number of men and women, boys and girls followed them to the outskirts of the city, cheering them on their way.

For forty days Ammon and his followers traveled in the wilderness in search of their brethren. They had seen no sign of them, so they began to feel discouraged and to think that their mission had been in vain. They did not know that at that time they were only a short distance from them, and that ere long they would be rejoicing in their company.

At the end of forty days' travel, Ammon and his brethren came to a high hill. At the foot of the hill they put up their tents. After having refreshed themselves, Ammon took three of his brethren and climbed to the top of the hill. When they reached the summit they saw a sight which brought the greatest joy to their hearts. In the valley below was a beautiful city, and in the city were their long-lost brethren.

Ammon and his comrades lost no time in making their way to the city. But just as they were about to enter it they were seized by several men—guards of the king—and taken off to prison. The men who arrested Ammon and his brethren did not know who they were: they thought they were spies sent out by the Lamanites.

The next day Ammon and his three companions were brought before King Limhi. The king asked them who they were, and when Ammon told him they were his brethren, and that they had come from Zarahemla in search of him and his people, Limhi rejoiced and praised the Lord. He sent out and brought the other members of Ammon's party into the city and treated them all with the greatest kindness.

The king then told Ammon all that had happened to the people of Zeniff from the time they had left their brethren: how they had broken the commandments of God and had killed the Prophet Abinadi. Because of that the Lord had forsaken them and had suffered them to be brought into bondage to the Lamanites.

"Well," said Ammon, "I feel that the Lord has sent us to deliver you and to lead you back to your own people in the land of Zarahemla."

King Limhi called his people together, and they listened with the greatest interest while Ammon told them that he and his brethren had come all the way from Zarahemla in search of them, and now that they had found them, they were going to help them to free themselves from bondage.

When Ammon had finished speaking, a man named Gideon, leader of the Nephite army, went forward and bowed down before the king. "O, king," said he, "if you will grant me permission I will undertake to deliver our people out of the power of the Lamanites."

"How do you think you can do that?" asked the king.

"In this way," said Gideon, "let all the people get ready for the journey, and tonight when the Lamanites are asleep I will lead our people out by the back pass. When the Lamanites awake in the morning we will be so far away that they cannot overtake us."

Gideon's plan pleased the king, and he at once gave orders to his people to prepare to make their escape. That night, while the Lamanites slept, Gideon got his people together, and, with Ammon and his brethren leading the way, they started for Zarahemla.

You can imagine the surprise of the Lamanites when they awoke the next morning and found the cities of the Nephites deserted. You can also imagine the surprise and joy of King Mosiah and the Nephites in Zarahemla when Ammon and his followers returned accompanied by their brethren and sisters who, through the power of God, had been delivered out of the hands of the Lamanites.

I suppose you would also like to know what became of Alma and his people, who made their escape from the army of King Noah. They settled in another part of the land and were doing well, when one day an army of Lamanites came down upon them and captured them and their city.

They also became servants to the Lamanites; but after a time the Lord helped them to make their escape, and they, too, came and joined their brethren in the land of Zarahemla.

REMARKABLE CONVERSIONS AND MISSIONARY EXPERIENCE.

After the Nephites had become reunited in Zarahemla, King Mosiah placed Alma at the head of the Church. Alma was a faithful servant of the Lord. He spent his time traveling through the land, teaching the Nephites the ways of the Lord and establishing branches of the Church among them.

For a number of years there was peace, happiness and prosperity in Zarahemla. Then a division took place among the people. Many of them ceased serving the Lord, left the Church, and began to persecute those who believed in and remained true to the faith of their fathers.

Among the unbelievers and persecutors were the four sons of King Mosiah, and a young man named Alma, the son of Alma who presided over the Church. The hearts of the parents of these young men were sorely grieved at the conduct of their sons. They did all in their power to turn them from their wicked course, but they utterly failed.

They refused, however, to give them up. They knew that where they had failed the Lord could succeed. So every day they knelt in prayer and pleaded with the Lord in behalf of their wayward and rebellious sons.

Let me tell you now what the prayers of these righteous parents accomplished. One day Alma the younger and the four sons of Mosiah decided to go to a certain place and make trouble for the Church there. They thought they were great fellows, and that they knew much more than did the people who belonged to the Church of God. But the Lord showed them that day how weak and ignorant they were, and how foolish it was for them to try to destroy the work which He had established.

What did the Lord do? He sent an angel from heaven to turn

these young men from their wicked course and to save them from destruction. Standing before Alma and the sons of Mosiah, the heavenly messenger spoke with a voice which caused the ground to tremble beneath their feet and Alma and his companions fell to the earth.

"The Lord has sent me to you," said the angel, "to tell you that you are doing a very wicked thing in persecuting His people and trying to destroy His Church. The Lord has great respect for your parents, for they are good people. He has heard their prayers in your behalf, and that is why He sent me to you. Now, you must repent of all the evil you have done, and turn to the Lord and serve Him faithfully all the days of your life."

After having delivered his message, the angel left them. Alma was so weak that he could not stand upon his feet, so the sons of Mosiah carried him to his father and told the elder Alma all that had happened.

On hearing the news, Alma's father rejoiced, and gave thanks to God for the great mercy which He had shown to his sons and also to the sons of Mosiah. He called a large number of people together and they fasted and prayed two days and two nights for Alma's recovery. At the end of that time his strength returned. He stood upon his feet and told the people all that the Lord had done for him.

From that time Alma and the sons of Mosiah became faithful workers in the Church, and were the means of turning many people to the Lord.

You will be interested, I know, in hearing of some remarkable things which took place while Alma was laboring as a missionary among certain of the Nephites who had departed from the true faith. What I am about to tell took place in one of the cities of the Nephites, called Ammonihah.

Alma had gone there alone to preach to the people. His mission was a hard one, for the people were very wicked. Day after day he stood up and preached to them, pleading with them to repent of their sins, that the judgments of God might not come upon them.

But they had become so wicked that the preaching of Alma had no effect upon them except to make them exceedingly angry and to cause them to treat the prophet in a shameful manner. They spat in his face, slapped him on the cheeks, and finally drove him out of the city.

We can imagine the feelings of the poor missionary as, with bowed head and sorrowful heart, he traveled along the road leading from Ammonihah to the city of Aaron. He believed when he first entered Ammonihah that he would find a few people at least who would give heed to what he said, and turn from their wicked ways; but, alas! he had not found one who was willing to do so. "Yes," thought he, "my mission has been a complete failure."

Just at that moment an angel of God descended from heaven and stood before him. He told Alma that he was the same heavenly messenger who had appeared to him and the sons of Mosiah some years before, and had converted them. The angel told Alma that the Lord was well pleased with him, because he had kept His commandments. He said also that the Lord wanted Alma to return to the city of Ammonihah and preach again to the people there.

The words of the heavenly visitor caused new joy and hope to spring up in Alma's heart. As soon as the angel had delivered his message, Alma turned and walked back towards the city from which he had been banished a short time before.

He was very weak and hungry, for he had fasted many days. As he was about to enter the city he met a man whom he stopped, and asked, "Will you give an humble servant of God something to eat?"

The man gazed on Alma with astonishment. Then he said, "Why, you are the man an angel told me about last night in a vision. I am very glad I have met you, for I know you are a true prophet of God."

The man's name was Amulek. He took Alma to his home, gave him food and drink, and made him rest several days. Then Alma and Amulek went out among the people and began to preach to them. They were filled with the spirit and power of God. To their great joy, many believed their message, repented of their sins, and began to live righteous lives.

But the greater part of the people would not believe the preaching of Alma and Amulek. They not only mocked the missionaries, but beat them and abused them in other shameful ways. Finally they seized Alma and Amulek and cast them into prison. They stripped them of all their clothing, bound them with strong cords, and kept them there for several days without either food or drink.

Each day a number of wicked men went to the prison and made mock of Alma and his companion. But that was not all: they also spat in their faces and slapped their cheeks.

The missionaries bore all these things with such patience that they astonished their enemies.

You might say, "Why did not the Lord come to the aid of His servants and deliver them out of the hands of those wicked men?"

Well, my children, that is just what He did do, as you will now hear.

One day a number of very bad men went to the prison in which the servants of the Lord were bound. They treated them in the same cruel manner as before. Suddenly the power of God rested mightily upon Alma and Amulek, and they sprang to their feet. "How long, Lord," cried Alma, "shall we suffer these great afflictions? O, Lord, give us strength, according to our faith which is in Christ, even unto our deliverance!" At that moment they broke the cords which bound them and stood free before their persecutors.

On seeing that, every one of the ungodly crowd began to tremble with fright. They tried to run out of the prison, but they could not. They were so overcome with fear that they fell on the prison floors. Then the Lord caused a terrible earthquake to shake the prison to its foundation, and a few moments later it was in a heap of ruins. Alma and Amulek walked out of the prison unharmed, but every one of the wicked men inside perished.

What a serious thing it is for people to persecute the servants of the living God.

MISSION OF THE SONS OF MOSIAH TO THE LAMANITES.

Some time after their conversion, Ammon, Aaron, Omner, and Himni, the four sons of Mosiah, requested their father to grant them permission to go to the land of Nephi, to preach the Gospel to the Lamanites there.

Mosiah prayed to the Lord concerning the matter, and the answer which he received was as follows: "Let them go up, for many shall believe on their words, and they shall have eternal life; and I will deliver thy sons out of the hands of the Lamanites."

This promise gave joy and encouragement to Mosiah and his sons. The day for the young men's departure came. They were joined by a number of faithful companions, and, with their father's blessing upon their heads, the little band of missionaries went forth "to seek and to save the lost."

That was one of the hardest missions ever undertaken by mortal man. The Lamanites in Nephi and surrounding places were a wild and wicked people. They took delight in murdering the Nephites and in stealing their property. They knew nothing concerning the true God, but worshiped idols. The Lord, however, had made a promise to the Lamanites that, through repentance, they would be blessed and given a knowledge of the true plan of salvation.

When the sons of Mosiah and their companions came to the land of the Lamanites they separated, each going to the place assigned him by Ammon, who was in charge of the company. Ammon chose as his field of labor the land of Ishmael. He had no sooner entered it than he was arrested by Lamanites, who bound him and confined him in a prison.

He was later brought before King Lamoni, who asked him if he were desirous of living with his people, the Lamanites. Ammon said he would be pleased to do so for a time, and that, perhaps, he might stay with them the rest of his life.

That pleased the king, and he ordered his servants to release Ammon. Lamoni told Ammon he would like him to marry one of his daughters, but the missionary respectfully declined. He told the king, however, that he would be his servant, and his offer was promptly accepted.

You might think that that was a strange thing for the missionary to do, and it was; but it was the right thing, as you will agree when you hear what took place a little later.

One day Ammon and a number of other servants of King Lamoni took their master's flocks to a certain place to water them. They had no sooner reached the place than a party of Lamanites came with their flocks. The latter began at once to make trouble for the king's servants by driving their flocks away and scattering them.

That was a very serious matter. The same thing had happened before to other servants of the king, and when they returned and told Lamoni what had taken place, he became very angry with them and ordered them to be put to death.

So, fearing that a similar fate might befall them, those who were with Ammon began to cry piteously. Ammon now saw an opportunity for him to exercise his powder, and he did so with good effect. He told his fellow-servants to dry their tears, and that he would help them to get the flocks together. He did so, but again the Lamanites began to drive them off.

Then Alma told his companions to look after the flocks while he went over to teach the Lamanites a lesson. He had not the least fear, for he remembered the promise which the Lord had made to his father—that He would deliver his sons out of the hands of the Lamanites.

The Lamanites laughed at one man coming out to oppose them, but their laughter was turned into mourning when six of their number lay dead upon the ground. With simple sling and stones Ammon fought his opponents single-handed, and, as I have said, slew six of them.

Seizing heavy clubs, a number of the Lamanites rushed at Ammon to kill him; but he was too smart for them. He grasped his sword and melded it with such skill that he slew their leader and also cut an arm off every man who raised his club against him. The rest fled in terror. Then Ammon returned, and, with his companions, attended to the watering of their master's flocks.

When King Lamoni heard what Ammon had done he was greatly astonished and exclaimed, "This is the Great Spirit, and he has come down at this time to preserve your lives, that I might not slay you as I did your brethren." "Where is Ammon?" the king asked, and when he was told that he was out attending to his majesty's horses, he said, "Surely there has not been any servant among all my servants that has been as faithful as this man; for even he doth remember all my commandments to execute them."

Lamoni sent for Amnion. He told him that he had heard of the wonderful thing which he had done, and asked him if he were the Great Spirit.

Ammon answered that he was not, that he was simply a servant of the true and living God. He told the king that he had not slain the Lamanites by his own power, but by the power which God had given Him.

The king requested Ammon to tell him about the true God whom he and his fathers worshiped. Ammon did so, and also explained to him the Gospel, pointing out to the king how he could obtain forgiveness of all his sins and at last be saved in the kingdom of God.

The king and queen of the Lamanites believed the things which Ammon told them, and they and many of their people were converted and baptized. The Lord bestowed great blessings upon them. King Lamoni had a vision, in which he beheld the Savior, and a number of others saw and conversed with angels. Then Ammon organized a branch of the Church amongst them, and had great joy at seeing the fruits of his missionary labors.

The Lord now made known to Ammon that three of his

missionary companions were in prison in the land of Middoni. Ammon told the news to the king, and added that he would have to go at once and do all in his power to have them released. The king said he would go with him and assist him.

On the way they met Lamoni's father, who was king over the whole land. The sight of his son riding in company with a Nephite threw the old king into a fit of fierce anger. He called Ammon all manner of vile names, and ordered his son to slay him. But, instead of doing so, Lamoni, to the astonishment of his father, stood up and defended Amnion. Lamoni's father drew his sword and rushed at Ammon to slay him, but Ammon smote him on the arm so that he could not use the weapon.

Finding himself at the mercy of Ammon, Lamoni's father pleaded with him to spare his life, saying if he would do so he would give him even to the half of his kingdom. "I will spare your life on these conditions," Ammon replied, "that you allow your son Lamoni to retain his kingdom, and that you have my brethren released from prison."

To that the old king willingly agreed. Ammon's brethren were given their liberty, and they and their companions traveled for years among the Lamanites preaching to them the everlasting Gospel. Thousands of the Lamanites were converted to the Lord, and they remained true to the faith all the days of their life. They became a kind and industrious people, and the Lord in His mercy took the curse away from them, so that they became white like the Nephites.

SAMUEL THE LAMANITE—HIS PROPHECIES AND THEIR FULFILLMENT.

I am going to tell you this evening about a great prophet who lived on this continent in the days of the Nephites. His name was Samuel. He was a Lamanite, but, because of his holy life, he was beloved of God, and was chosen to be a prophet unto His people.

Through the blessings of the Lord and their own industry the Nephites in Zarahemla became exceedingly wealthy. Then, like many others, before and since, they allowed pride and other corrupt feelings to enter into their hearts and to drive out the love for God and His righteousness which had held place there for years.

As their good works had won for them the favor and blessings of God, so their wickedness was fast bringing upon them His condemnation and punishment. In order to save them from destruction, the Lord sent Samuel the Lamanite to plead with them to repent of their sins and to turn again into the way of righteousness from which they had wandered.

Day after day the voice of the prophet was heard among the Nephites crying repentance, and prophesying concerning great and wonderful things which would take place in the future. I am going to tell you about a remarkable prophecy which he uttered at that time, and which was fulfilled to the very letter.

Standing upon the top of a high wall, so that many of the people could see and hear him, Samuel prophesied of a wonderful event which he said would take place five years from that time. It would be the greatest event in history—the birth of Jesus, the Savior of the world.

It was to take place in another country, near the city in which Lehi and his family lived before they set out for the promised land. The prophet told them of certain signs which would be given at the time of the Savior's birth. When they saw the signs they might know that the Son of God had come into the world to redeem mankind from sin and death.

These were some of the signs: the night before the Lord would be born there would be no darkness at all; the night would be just as bright and clear as the day had been; a new star, one that had never been seen before, would make its appearance in the heavens. The prophet said that when these signs would be given many of the people would be so astonished and overcome that they would fall to the earth.

Then Samuel the Lamanite prophesied concerning the Savior's life—that He would be despised and rejected of men—and also concerning His death and resurrection. He told the people that at the time the Savior would be put to death, neither the sun, moon, nor stars would give any light, so that on this continent there would be continuous darkness for three days and nights. There would also be terrible tempests, and earthquakes which would shake the earth, cause the mountains to fall, and many cities to be destroyed.

Then the warning voice of the prophet was heard again, calling upon the Nephites to repent of their sins, that they might escape the judgments of God.

You will be glad to hear that many of the people who heard Samuel believed his words. They repented sincerely of their wickedness and were baptized for the remission of their sins. Others, however, became angry, and tried to take the prophet's life by throwing stones and shooting arrows at him as he stood upon the wall.

Strange to tell, the servant of the Lord was not hit once, although rocks and arrows flew round him in great numbers. On seeing how Samuel was protected by the power of God, many more of the Nephites were converted, and, through repentance and baptism, were restored to the Church of Christ.

Then the cry went up from the ungodly ones, "Take this fellow and bind him, for behold he hath a devil; and because of the power of the devil which is in him, we cannot hit him with our stones and our arrows; therefore take him and bind him, and away with him."

They began to climb the wall, but before they had reached the top, Samuel had jumped down on the other side and made his escape. He was never seen again by the Nephites.

Five years passed by. The time had now come for the fulfillment of the first part of Samuel the Lamanite's prophecy—the time of the Savior's birth. Then the wicked and unbelieving among the Nephites arose and said that the time was past, that the signs had not appeared, that Samuel was a false prophet, and that all who believed on him should be put to death. They decided, however, before carrying out their threat, to name a certain day on which the signs should appear. If that day should pass without the signs being given, then the believers among the Nephites might prepare for the fate which had been decreed against them.

Among the faithful was a man named Nephi. He believed every word that Samuel the Lamanite had spoken. The day before the one set apart by the unbelievers Nephi went out and prayed for hours unto the Lord in behalf of his people. Then the voice of the Lord came unto him, saying, "Be of good cheer, for behold the time is at hand, and on this night shall the sign be given, and on the morrow come I into the world."

His heart filled with joy and gladness, Nephi returned and told the good news to his brethren and sisters, and they rejoiced and praised the Lord.

To the great astonishment of all the unbelievers, that night the signs were given—there was no darkness, but the night was just as bright as the midday before. The new star appeared, and then, just as the prophet had predicted, many of the wicked fell to the earth, being overcome with fear because of their iniquities. The spirit of repentance took possession of the great majority of the unbelievers; they were converted, baptized, and made members of the Church.

About thirty-four years later some terrible things took place in this land. For three days and nights the whole country was enveloped in darkness. So great was the darkness that it was impossible for the people to strike a light or kindle a fire. Then a frightful storm burst forth, the like of which had never been seen in all the land. The thunders of heaven shook the earth and lightning set fire to many cities, among them the great city of Zarahemla. Mountains fell, cities were buried, and others sank in the depths of the sea.

All that terrible destruction took place at the time the Savior was put to death on the cross outside of Jerusalem. It had come upon the people just as Samuel the Lamanite had predicted, as a punishment for their sins.

Then followed a time of weeping and mourning among those whose lives had been spared. In anguish of soul they cried, "O, that we had repented before this great and terrible day, and had not killed the prophets and cast them out. Then none of these things would have come upon us."

In the midst of their heart-rending lamentations a voice was heard from heaven. It was the voice of Jesus. "Behold," said He, "I am Jesus Christ, the Son of God. I created the heavens and the earth, and all things that in them are." The Savior told them that He had finished the mission which His Father had given Him. He called upon them to repent and to be baptized, promising them, if they would do so, a remission of their sins and the gift of the Holy Ghost.

The words of the blessed Redeemer brought peace and consolation to their souls. They willingly yielded obedience to His Divine commands, and the blessings of the Lord were bestowed upon them in rich abundance.

TWO MEMORABLE BATTLES.

The Lamanites throughout the land who had not been converted preserved in their hearts a deadly hatred towards the Nephites. Time after time the Lamanites made war upon the Nephites, and tens of thousands of lives were sacrificed on both sides.

If I were to begin to tell you the terrible results of their wars, before I had proceeded far you would put your fingers in your ears and cry, "Stop! stop! stop!"

I am going to tell you of two of their battles. A remarkable thing happened in connection with one of them which, when you have heard it, will show you some of the wonderful things which can be accomplished through faith.

The Lamanites who were converted through the preaching of the sons of Mosiah were afterwards known as the people of Ammon. They left their own lands and went to reside in a place called Jershon, not far from Zarahemla. They entered into a covenant with the Lord that they would never take up arms against their Lamanite brethren.

Now, there were a great many of the Nephites who had broken the commandments of God. Because of that, they had lost their membership in the Church, and were not numbered among the people of the Lord. That was a terrible thing. But their condition became much worse when they turned traitors, joined themselves to the Lamanites, and began to fight against their Nephite brethren.

The chief captain over the armies of the Nephites at that time was a young man named Moroni. He Avas a God-fearing man, and a prophet. He was also a great general. In time of peace he prepared for war. He provided his soldiers with thick clothing, with breast-plates, head-plates and arm-plates, as protection against the deadly weapons of the Lamanites.

The Lamanite armies had at their head a man named Zarahemna. He was a great soldier, too. But he had not thought of protecting his men as Moroni had protected his. The Lamanite soldiers were naked, except for a girdle of skin, which they wore about their loins.

Moroni heard that the Lamanites were coming to make war upon his people. He, therefore, got his armies ready to meet them. Feeling confident of an easy victory, the Lamanites marched towards the land of Jershon. As they drew near it they saw Moroni's army prepared to oppose them. Seeing how well the Nephite soldiers were protected, the Lamanites changed their minds, and instead of attacking Jershon they turned and proceeded towards the land of Manti.

Moroni did not know where the Lamanites were going, so he sent out spies to watch them. He also sent a messenger to Alma to request the prophet to ask the Lord to reveal to him the movements of the Lamanites. The Lord told Alma they were marching towards the land of Manti.

On hearing that, Moroni left part of his army in Jershon, to protect that place, and with the rest he hastened to Manti, arriving there some time ahead of the Lamanites. He called to his assistance all the men in Manti who could bear arms, and when the Lamanites again appeared Moroni was ready to give them battle.

The war commenced. Both sides fought with all the courage and fierceness they could command. Several times the Lamanites were driven back, and each time they returned to the conflict. The slaughter which took place is terrible to read about. Before the war was half over, thousands of lives had been sacrificed.

At one time the Nephites showed signs of weakening. Then the voice of General Moroni rang out, reminding his men of that for which they were fighting—their religion, their liberty, their wives and children, their houses and lands. His words filled their hearts with renewed courage, and with a cry to the Lord to help them, the Nephites rushed upon the Lamanites and slew them in great numbers. Seeing that his enemies were beaten, Moroni commanded his men to stop slaying them.

Addressing Zerahemna, Moroni said, "You see now that you are in our power. It would be easy for us to slay you, but we do not desire to shed your blood. I, therefore, call upon you and your followers to deliver unto us your weapons of war, and to enter into a covenant that you will never again take up arms against us. If you refuse to do this, I will command my men to attack you again and utterly destroy you."

When Moroni had finished speaking, Zerahemna stepped forward and handed him his sword, cimeter and bow. "We are willing," he said, "to surrender to your our weapons, but we will not enter into a covenant never to go to war with you again, because we know we would not keep our promise."

On hearing that, Moroni handed Zerahemna back his weapons and the deadly conflict was resumed. The Lord gave great strength to the Nephites so that the Lamanites fell before them in large numbers. At last Zerahemna began to plead for mercy, so Moroni gave orders for the battle to cease. The conquered Lamanites laid down their arms at the feet of the Nephites, and after entering into the covenant proposed by Moroni, they were permitted to return to their own lands.

Peace reigned throughout the land for a number of years. Then the Lamanites broke the covenant they had made with the Nephites and a series of terrible wars followed.

Several times the people of Ammon (the Lamanites whom Ammon and his brethren had converted) were tempted to break their covenant with the Lord and to take up arms in defense of the Nephites. They refrained, however, from doing so.

But among the people of Ammon there were two thousand young men who were little boys when their fathers made covenant with the Lord that they would never fight against their Lamanite brethren. These young men had not made such a promise, so they came forward and offered their services to the Nephites—to help them preserve their religion, their liberty, their houses and lands.

Their kind offer was willingly accepted. They chose as their leader a man named Helaman. No father was ever more proud of his sons than was Helaman of his two thousand young soldiers. And well he might be, for no better army ever entered a field of battle. Besides their weapons of war, they were armed with a far greater thing—a perfect faith in God. That faith had been planted in their hearts through the teachings of their godly mothers. They had been taught from their childhood to have implicit faith in the Lord, and to tryst Him in every hour of trial.

One day these two thousand young soldiers found themselves engaged in battle with a large army of the Lamanites. The lighting was terrible on both sides. Helaman and his little army fought like dragons. Many of the Lamanites were slain, and finally the remainder threw down their arms and offered themselves as prisoners of war.

The battle ended, Helaman proceeded to call the roll of his army, and to his great astonishment every one of his two thousand young warriors answered "Present."

"Not one of them was killed!"

No, not a single one. Their faith had saved them.

CHRIST'S VISIT TO THE NEPHITES.

One day a large number of Nephites were assembled at the temple in the land Bountiful. It was soon after the terrible destruction I told you about in a former story, and the people were talking about the great changes which had taken place.

Suddenly the whole multitude was startled by a strange voice speaking to them out of heaven. It was neither a loud nor a harsh voice, but it was so powerful that it thrilled the hearts of all who heard it. The voice was heard twice, but no one understood the words which were spoken.

As the people stood looking up towards heaven, the voice spoke to them again, and that time they understood the heavenly message. It was the voice of God. "Behold," said He, "my beloved Son, in whom I am well pleased, in whom I have glorified my name; hear ye him."

At that moment the heavens were opened and a glorious personage, clothed in a robe of spotless white, descended and stood in the midst of the people. Every eye was turned upon Him. He stretched forth His hand and there was perfect silence. Then He addressed the multitude, saying, "Behold, I am Jesus Christ, whom the prophets testified shall come into the world."

They listened with almost breathless interest while He told them of the mission which He had performed and of the cruel death which He had suffered upon the cross. He showed them the wounds which the nails had made in His hands and feet and which the sword had made in His side. He invited them to come forward one by one and feel the prints of the nails and the mark of the sword.

They all did as He desired. Then with united voice they exclaimed, "Hosanna! blessed be the name of the Most High God." And they fell down at the feet of Jesus and worshiped Him.

The Savior bade Nephi to come to Him. The faithful disciple went forward, and kneeling upon the ground, kissed the feet of his beloved Redeemer. The Lord gave Nephi authority to baptize, as He also did to a number of others whom He chose from among the assembly. He gave them instructions concerning the manner in which they were to baptize people, and told them the words they should use when performing the ordinance.

When repentant believers came to be baptized they were to be taken down into the water. Then, calling them by name, the person appointed to perform the ordinance should say, "Having authority given me of Jesus Christ, I baptize you in the name of the Father, and of the Son, and of the Holy Ghost. Amen. And then," said Jesus, "ye shall immerse them in the water, and come forth again out of the water."

For a long time the Savior stood up in the midst of the Nephites teaching them the glorious principles of the everlasting Gospel. Then He told them to go to their homes, but to meet again on the morrow, when He would pay them another visit and give them further instructions.

But they had no desire to go away. They stood looking pleadingly at the Lord, wishing in their hearts that He would tarry with them a little longer. Tears were coursing down their cheeks, and on seeing His people weeping, the Savior was filled with compassion for them.

He asked them if there were any sick among them, and on being told there were many. He requested that they be brought to Him. At His Divine command the blind received their sight, the lame were made to walk, and the sick were restored to perfect health. So grateful were those who were healed that they knelt down before the Lord, kissed His feet and bathed them with their tears.

Jesus then told the Nephites to bring their little children to Him. They did so. He requested all present to kneel with Him upon the ground. Then the voice of the Lord was heard in prayer, and so marvelous were the words which He uttered that no one was permitted to make a record of them. After prayer, the Savior blessed each of the little ones, when immediately the heavens were opened and angels came down and ministered unto them.

Christ then instituted the sacrament among the Nephites, and, after giving them much good counsel, He dismissed them. That was the most glorious day in the history of the Nephites. When we read of the wonderful things which took place on that occasion the wish arises in our hearts that we had been there, to behold the face of our resurrected Lord, and to hear the glorious truths which fell from His libs.

THE THREE NEPHITES.

After ministering to the Nephites, Jesus returned to His Father in Heaven. Then the people went to their homes. The news of the Savior's visit, and of the wonderful things which He had done, was carried to all the Nephites. There were many of them who did not go to bed that night. They had to get ready for the next day, for the Lord had promised the Nephites that He would visit them again on the morrow.

The day following, when all the people had assembled together, there were so many that they had to be divided into twelve bodies. Jesus had chosen twelve disciples to preside over the Nephites and to teach them the Gospel. These ministers of the Lord knelt down with the people upon the ground and prayed with all their hearts to God for the gift of His Holy Spirit. Their prayers were answered. They not only received the Holy Spirit, but angels came down from heaven and ministered unto them.

Then, to the great joy of all the people, Jesus descended and stood in their midst. He requested them to kneel down upon the ground, and when they had done so the Lord and His disciples prayed for them. When their prayers were ended the people arose. Jesus brought forth bread and wine and they all partook of the sacrament. The Savior remained with them a long time, teaching them many glorious principles—things which you, my children, will learn as you grow in years.

One day the twelve disciples whom Jesus had chosen met together to fast and pray. While thus engaged in worshiping God, the Lord appeared in their midst. He asked them what they would like Him to do for them after He had returned to His Father.

Nine of them said the desire of their hearts was that, after having fulfilled their mission on earth, they might be permitted to go to the Lord in His kingdom. Jesus was pleased with their request, and He told the nine that when they were seventy-two years old He would take them to heaven, to live in peace and happiness forever.

The Lord then turned to the three disciples who had not spoken. He asked them what they desired Him to do for them. They did not answer Him, for they were afraid to tell Him the desire that was in their hearts.

But Jesus knew their thoughts. He told them they desired to have power over death, that they might live till He would come in His glory, and spend their days in the service of God. The Lord blessed them, and promised them that they should never taste of death, neither would they have any more pain or sorrow.

Jesus touched the three Nephites with His finger, and then left them. Immediately the heavens were opened, and the three disciples were caught up into heaven, where they saw and heard many wonderful things. Later they appeared again on earth and began to teach the people the things which the Savior had commanded them.

These three men were the greatest of all the Nephites. They were filled with the Spirit and power of God, and death had no power over them. One time they were cast into prison. They commanded the prison to fall, and, to the astonishment of all the people, the prison fell, but the three Nephites walked forth unharmed.

On another occasion they were cast into a furnace, but the fire had no effect upon them; they came out unhurt. Then they were thrown into a den of wild beasts. Their persecutors expected to see them devoured immediately, but, to their great surprise, the beasts became as gentle as lambs and the three disciples played with them.

I suppose you would like to know what became of the three Nephites. I believe they are still on the earth. They are to minister among all nations, without being known, and shall perform great and mighty works before the Lord shall come.

THE REIGN OF PEACE.

I am going to tell you this evening of some of the great blessings which came to the Nephites, after the visit of the Savior to them. The twelve disciples whom Jesus had chosen established the true Church in all parts of the land. It was called the Church of Christ. The Lord told His disciples that that was to be the name of the Church.

In order to become a member of the Church, a person had to repent of his sins. He had to confess to the Lord that he had broken His commandments, that he felt sorry for having done so, and that in future he would live a good life.

Then he would be ready for baptism. A man, who had authority to baptize, would take him down into a pond or river. He would call the person by name, and repeat the words which the Lord had told His servants to use: "Having authority given me of Jesus Christ, I baptize you in the name of the Father, and of the Son, and of the Holy Ghost. Amen." Then he would immerse him in the water and bring him up again out of the water.

By obedience to these commandments of the Lord, the person was cleansed from all his sins, and became pure and holy in the sight of God. Then the elders of the Church would place their hands upon his head and confirm him a member of the Church, and say, "Receive ye the Holy Ghost."

The Lord was highly pleased with His people. They all loved each other, and took delight in helping one another. The elders of the Church had great power. They were able, through the help of the Lord, to heal the sick, open the eyes of the blind, cause the lame to walk, and even raise the dead.

The Lamanites were converted also, and became members of the Church of Christ. All the ill-feeling which they had towards the Nephites was taken out of their hearts and the love of God took its place. Instead of going to war with the Nephites, they went to Church with them, and united in praising God for the great blessings which He had given them.

Those were the happiest days the Nephites and Lamanites had ever known. All the people were just like the members of one family. There were no rich nor poor among them, but all were equal. I will tell you how they came to be in that condition.

When the Church was established, all the members who had money brought it to the authorities and had it put into a common fund. All that was made after that was put into the same fund, and each family received from time to time the amount needed for its support. So, you see, that made the people equal in temporal things as well as in spiritual things.

Through keeping the commandments of God, the Nephites became very strong and very beautiful. They married and raised families. They scattered all over the land and built up many fine cities. The farms yielded abundance of food for man and beast and the orchards were laden with fruit in the season thereof.

Every man dealt honestly with his neighbor. There was neither lying, nor stealing, nor murdering, nor any kind of wickedness known among the people. They loved the Lord and kept His commandments, and the Lord loved them and poured down His blessings upon them without measure. In that blessed state the Nephites lived for over one hundred and eighty years.

Soon after that time a terrible change took place, which I will tell you about in my next—my last—story.

THE LAST OF THE NEPHITES.

For almost two hundred years after the Savior's appearance among them, the Nephites lived in a state of perfect peace and happiness. It seemed as if heaven and earth had been joined together. From time to time angels came down and ministered unto the people, bringing them glad tidings from the Lord.

Then certain of the Nephites began to do things which were displeasing in the sight of God. They did not attend to their prayers as they had done, neither did they go to the house of the Lord on the Sabbath day to worship Him. They made mock of sacred things and persecuted those who remained true to the faith.

The Lord took His Holy Spirit out of the hearts of those wicked people. He also took the three Nephites away from them. He would not suffer His servants to preach to them, for they had become so bad that they could not be brought to repentance.

Then the Lamanites began to make war upon the Nephites. There was a young man among the Nephites whose name was Mormon. He had led an upright, godly life, and possessed great faith and courage. He was chosen to lead the Nephite army.

Mormon armed his men and got them in readiness to meet the Lamanites. The day of battle at last arrived. An army of fifty thousand Lamanites came down upon the Nephites. In Mormon's army there were only thirty thousand men. Before the battle commenced Mormon addressed his soldiers. "Men," said he, "be of good courage, the victory will be ours. Remember, it is for your wives and your children, your homes and your lands that you go out to fight this day."

On hearing those inspiring words the heart of every soldier in the Nephite ranks was filled with renewed courage. With swords unsheathed they marched forth boldly to meet the foe. The battle commenced. How long it raged I know not, but the Lamanites were finally beaten and driven back with considerable loss. The Nephites regained possession of their own lands, and lived in peace for a number of years.

Their victories over the Lamanites, instead of teaching the Nephites humility, caused them to become proud and boastful. They did not give any glory to God for the success which had come to them. They said it was by their own strength they had defeated their enemies, and declared they would fight the Lamanites till they had utterly destroyed them.

Mormon went among his people time after time and pleaded with them to turn from their evil ways. He knew that if they did not do so the judgments of God would come upon them. They paid no attention to his pleadings, so he told them they could get another man to take charge of their armies, as he would no longer act as their general.

The Lord saw that the Nephites did not appreciate the blessings which He had bestowed upon them, and that they had no desire to serve Him. He, therefore, turned away from them and left them to fight their own battles.

Again the Lamanites armed themselves and proclaimed war against the Nephites. Feeling confident of victory, the Nephites entered the field of battle. But the Lord was not on their side, so they met with a terrible defeat.

Other battles were fought, in which tens of thousands of Nephites were slain. I cannot describe the sorrow of Mormon when he saw the awful destruction which had been wrought among his people. He determined to make another effort to save them. He again took charge of their armies and went forth to meet the Lamanites. That was the last battle between the Nephites and Lamanites. It was fought in the vicinity of the hill Cumorah, and ended in the entire destruction of the Nephites, save one.

That man was named Moroni. He was the son of Mormon, and, like his father, was a lover of righteousness. Moroni hid himself from the Lamanites. He finished the history of his people, and then he, at the command of the Lord, deposited it in the hill Cumorah.

There it lay for hundreds and hundreds of years. At last the time came for it to be brought forth. Then the Lord sent His servant Moroni to a young man named Joseph Smith, to tell him of the precious history which had been kept from the world so long.

Four years later, Joseph was given the sacred record. By the power of God he translated it into the English language. That record is the Book of Mormon, from which I have taken these stories. May our Heavenly Father sanctify them to your good, my children, is my prayer, in the name of Jesus Christ. Amen.

www.ingramcontent.com/pod-product-compliance
Lightning Source LLC
Chambersburg PA
CBHW022120090426
42743CB00008B/937